Forthright & Steadfast

Forthright & Steadfast

The Wooden Fishing Boats of Richard Irvin & Sons

GLORIA WILSON

Published 2017 by
Lodestar Books
71 Boveney Road, London, SE23 3NL, United Kingdom
lodestarbooks.com

Copyright © Gloria Wilson 2017
The right of Gloria Wilson to be identified as the author of this work has been asserted by her in accordance with the Copyright, Designs and Patents Act 1988

All rights reserved

A CIP catalogue record for this book is available from the British Library

ISBN 978-1-907206-41-2

Typeset by Lodestar Books in Equity designed by Matthew Butterick

Printed in Spain by Graphy Cems, Navarra

All papers used by Lodestar Books are sourced responsibly

Contents

	Foreword	9
	Introduction	13
1	Sleek and Elegant	15
2	Capacious	19
3	Wise Artisanship	23
4	Remarkable Run of Affairs	27
5	Heady Days	32
	Illustrations	37
	Afterword: Contradistinctive	136
	Acknowledgements	138

List of Illustrations

1–2	*Silver Hope*	51–53	*Sparkling Star*
3–5	*Star of Peace*	54 (a,b,c)	*Enterprise*
6–7	*Fear Not*	55–58	Peterhead scenes
8	*Fragrance*	59–60	*Reliant*
9	*West*ward	61–64	*Star Crest*
10	*Graceful*	65	*Fishing News* advertisement for pair-trawl gear
11	*Glenugie III*	66	*Ulysses*
12	*Hamnavoe*	67	*Achieve*
13	*Ocean Crest* landing herring	68	*Sunbeam*
14–16	*Prevail*	69	*Resplendent* & *Sunbeam* construction
17–21	*Vigilant*	70–73	*Resplendent*
22–24	*Achilles*	74–75	*Graceful*
25	*Utilise*	76–77	*Daisy*
26	*Stanhope II* & *Ugievale II* construction	78	*A Sea Street Anthology*
27–29	*Stanhope II*	79	*Replenish* & *Radiant Way* fitting out
30	*Ugievale II* in frame	80–81	*Replenish*
31	*Ugievale II*	82–83	*Radiant Way*
32	*Forthright* & *Steadfast*	84	*Duncairn*
33–36	*Forthright*	85	*Constant Friend*
37	*Forthright* record catch at Peterhead, 1973	86	*Sunbeam* construction
38	*Forthright* unloading catch	87–90	*Sunbeam*
39–42	*Steadfast*	91	*Rambler Rose*
43–44	*Forthright* & *Steadfast* lines	92	Peterhead fish market *c*1972
45	Half-model	93	Aberdeen fish market 1972
46–47	Lofting	94	Aberdeen quayside with 'side-winders'
48–49	Making frame templates	95	Irvin advertisement in *Fishing News*, 1973
50	Hull section notes	page 137	*Ben Asdale*

Foreword

In *Forthright & Steadfast* Gloria Wilson illuminates the work of the Richard Irvin shipyard in Peterhead on Scotland's east coast between the years 1950 and 1978, when the company ceased new construction. She marks its passing and the end of an era that in my view deserves to be marked and celebrated far more than it is. It is a fact that those of us born in the mid twentieth century have been witness to the final blooming of a thousand-year-old tradition in the British Isles, that of commercial wooden shipbuilding. It has gone extinct in our generation and is unlikely ever to return.

We are not talking wooden boatbuilding here which continues to thrive in a modest way in the world of yachts, adapting as it does so to modern methods and materials. No, what is described in these pages is a different world altogether. In the first place it is a commercial world in which the economic equation of return on investment drives both vessel design and construction. They in turn are a reflection of continual changes in fishing methods, engine power and equipment. Secondly, it is the world of heavy timber construction in which vessels are built on sawn frames of massive proportion cut from grown oak, that is, from the natural crooks of the English oak tree, and are planked with larch, spiked on with galvanised boat nails, the seams caulked with cotton and oakum. It's a method little changed from that used by the Elizabethan explorers, or by the Royal Navy in the Napoleonic wars, or by the East India company in the age of colonisation. That it survived in the fishing industry long after it had died out in all other areas of marine trade is a remarkable fact.

More remarkable still, at the same time Neil Armstrong was landing on the moon, one could walk into boatyards all round the coast of Britain and see this ancient art being practiced, not out of sentimentality, but because it was still the best solution to the economic equation. In larger vessels wood gave way to steel in the early years of the last century, but steel was slow to find its way down to small and medium size fishing vessels. Fishermen prized the cleanliness and relative ease of maintenance of a wooden boat and the weight distribution in the structure that has so much to do with motion at sea. In the 1970s fibreglass broke through into the smaller end of the commercial sector and began steadily working its way up into the ground traditionally held by wood boats. Caught between the two alternative materials, heavy wood finally succumbed in the last decades of the twentieth century, its demise hurried along by the fishing policies of the European Union. I cannot say for sure that no wooden fishing vessels are being built today in the British Isles, but if they are, they will be the exceptions. The last generation of craftsmen steeped in this tradition, along with the specialist suppliers of grown timber and fastenings, are all sinking below the horizon now. This is what makes this book so valuable and so timely.

Gloria Wilson grew up in an artistic family in Staithes on the Yorkshire coast and it was there that she became interested in the small fleet of English cobles. Later, in nearby Whitby, she first encountered the lovely Scottish cruiser sterned vessels that seem to have cast a spell over her entire working life.

I discovered Gloria's work in the 1970s as a young naval architect doing stability work on a wooden fishing vessel under construction in Cornwall in south-west England. Having grown up in a boatyard I was familiar enough with wooden boats, but the heavy sawn frame construction used in fishing boat building was a different planet and a revelation to me. I read everything I could on the subject, from the scantling rules of the White Fish Authority which prescribe the dimensions of all structural members, to Gloria Wilson's books *Scottish Fishing Craft* and *More Scottish Fishing Craft*, and her many articles in *Fishing News,* as well as the writings of the great Ayrshire builder Alexander Noble. There they are on my bookshelf now in a well used section that includes the standard texts on fishing vessel stability—a reminder of a very happy period in my life

It was no coincidence that my focus at that time was north of the border. It was clear that the Scots were on the leading edge of things. It was the Scots who were pushing the limits of the length/beam ratio, building boats wider and with greater freeboard than ever before. How it must have distressed Gloria to see her beloved cruiser stern give way to transoms, but that was the trend—and still is. Increased engine power and the explosion of hydraulically operated equipment changed the picture too, adding loads to the structure never envisaged by the authors of the White Fish Authority rules. In response the Scottish builders were incorporating ever more steel into their vessels—engine beds, bulkheads and deck support knees. Gloria's description of the Irvin shop filled with a mixture of smoke from the welders and steam from the steam box used to soften and bend the planking captures the era perfectly.

Another milestone she notes is the imposition of stability regulations and assessment both before construction begins and after launch—this as a direct result of the development of computer software in the early 1970s. No longer were the builder's model and the loftsman's eye sufficient warranty of seaworthiness, as they had been for all previous generations. From here on every step of the process would bear the regulator's stamp. That was a big change, and while probably for the best, one feels for those quiet competent tradesmen Gloria so admires—men with more intuitive knowledge than an army of mathematicians.

The best parts of the book from my point of view are the descriptions of the method used at Irvin's to evolve their designs from one boat to the next. Her portrait of George McKechnie the loftsman is priceless. I could have wished for much more of that kind of conversation with the tradesmen in the yard to better understand their methods and equipment. But one cannot have it all. Gloria's vision is a wide one that includes the development of the port of Peterhead, the skippers and their landings as well as her experiences going to sea in the vessels she so loved.

Gloria Wilson truly belongs in the tradition of the folklorists—individuals moved initially by the discovery of beauty in the commonplace who are then compelled to understand and record what they find. In doing so they leave a legacy of riches for future generations. In that sense she keeps company with the likes of Cecil Sharp and Alan Lomax, or in the world of boats, Phillip Oke and Howard Chapelle. One hopes her example will spur others to similar effort, for the capturing of culture and local knowledge before it slips away is always a noble pursuit.

Paul Gartside
Long Island NY
August 2017

Introduction

Scottish wooden-hulled cruiser-sterned fishing boats have always been appreciated for their seakindly characteristics. They are such superb shapes, with tremendous functional beauty and aesthetic appeal, and are among the most highly respected and adaptable fishing vessel types built during the twentieth century.

In the 1950s, eleven boatbuilding yards along the stretch of coast from Peterhead to Buckie produced between them as many as fifty to sixty such boats each year. This is in dramatic contrast to fewer than a dozen built in the same area during the whole of the 1980s, by which time the more spacious transom stern had taken over.

Consisting of a sharp-ended counter which rakes forward at the centreline, the cruiser stern has its fullest part at, or just above, the waterline. It affords good manoeuvrability for working the flydragging seine net, which had been developed by the Scots in the 1920s for catching haddock, whiting, cod, lemon sole and plaice, on or close to the seabed, and was still a principal fishing method in that country fifty years later. Rudder and propeller were tucked underneath, leaving the stern free of obstruction for working the seine net.

One of the most respected builders of cruiser-sterned fishing boats was Richard Irvin & Sons Ltd., in Peterhead, north of Aberdeen. This book is my personal celebration of some of the larger vessels built there between 1950 and 1978, after which the company withdrew from boatbuilding.

Because the book reflects my particular experience, enthusiasms, and first hand research, and the photographs and drawings are my own work, it must of necessity leave some gaps. I was not there all the time. I have chosen to focus on the boats which I knew the best, which I met during visits to Peterhead, or watched under construction in the Irvin shed where I saw wise artisanship of a high order.

In common with many Scottish builders of wooden fishing boats, Irvin's design techniques were based more on art, intuition and personal opinion than on the science of naval architecture, and without the opportunity to test and analyse the performance of scale models, or the actual boats, for factors such as seakindliness and resistance. This was, nevertheless, a sound development of a series of boats which have proved themselves in rough seas over many years.

Fishermen regard their vessels as individual beings, and discuss their merits and peculiarities in critical detail. Boats become part of a fisherman's essentialness, his spirit and frame of mind, and are things of great enchantment.

For me, too, some of these agreeable Irvin vessels formed a constant thread, a leitmotif, through my life for a number of years. And I had trips to sea with some of them.

I studied painting and drawing at Durham University, and gained a BA (Hons) in Fine Art, and so I feel that drawings can sometimes go beyond the photograph as a means of exploring and understanding the boats, and perhaps reaching even more deeply into their intrinsic qualities.

And I was thrilled to discover that one of Scotland's leading and most original twentieth-century artists also looked upon the Irvin boats as worthwhile subject matter.

Gloria Wilson
October 2016

1 Sleek and Elegant

From 1953 to 1978 Irvin built fifty wooden-hulled carvel-planked cruiser-sterned vessels more than 70ft in length. Their style evolved from slender narrow-gutted boats 72ft and 73ft long with 19ft 6in beam, to capacious gutsy full-bodied craft the largest of which measured 85ft with beam of 24ft.

Subtle alterations were often made to the shapes of successive boats. These were arrived at by critical assessment of those already fishing, and to comply with each new vessel's equipment and proposed fishing methods, and the preferences of her owners. Modifications from boat to boat may have been small but, over a period of time, they amounted to quite significant changes.

Peterhead had been an important herring port since the early nineteenth century owing to the nearness of rich fishing grounds. During the 1950s local fishermen began to dispose of their obsolete steam-powered herring drifters, and Irvin built about half a dozen large, economical motor boats, designed primarily for herring drifting and great-line fishing. They delighted the fishermen, being ideal replacements to the steam driven vessels.

Drift nets could stretch for upwards of a mile, and were hung vertically in the path of on-coming fish, which were caught in the mesh by their gills. The drifter lay bow to the nets for several hours before starting to haul. Herring swam in colossal shoals sometimes ten miles long, and bigger catches were often made when the moon was full or there was a bit of a breeze. Great-lines were lengths of thin rope with baited hooks attached at intervals, and were used to catch large cod, ling, halibut and skate on rocky ground.

Built in 1954, *Silver Hope* PD377, later FR29, typified the large 1950s Irvin drifter-liner. A sleek, elegant boat 73ft long with 19ft 6in beam, she was powered by a Gardner 152 horsepower diesel engine and fitted with a mechanically driven winch. She had easy sheer, straight stem, and rounded forefoot, long straight keel with drag, moderate rise of floor with hollow, or 'tuck', in the garboards, fairly hard bilges and a cruiser stern.

In the 1990s I spoke to naval architect Maurice Napier about the main design features of this type of boat. 'The deep draught aft was for seakindliness and to accommodate the propeller aperture, and they had a hollow run for speed', he told me. 'A deep draught forward would help course-keeping but was bad for manoeuvrability, so a happy medium had to be found here. The rounded forefoot was also a compromise between a large radius for manoeuvrability and a small radius for course keeping.

'Tuck helped seakindliness and gave effectively a deeper keel which resisted sideways movement and reduced rolling. They had a fairly full midships section but the ends were also full in order to reduce pitching and keep the deck dry. The cruiser stern could be an advantage in a following sea. With changes in fishing methods and an increase in top weight these boats have become fuller and beamier with deeper draught and more freeboard and greater buoyancy. Their bilges are harder and floors flatter with less tuck and they have larger propeller apertures.'

During the 1950s herring shoals became erratic and scarce. Peterhead fishermen turned more to flydragging seine net fishing for demersal species, using a conical net attached to the boat by long ropes. Demersal fish are those living on or close to the sea bed. As the seiner moves ahead she slowly hauls the ropes, which converge and shepherd the fish into the path of the net.

Seining required stouter, more buoyant and powerful boats, with additional deck space for carrying nets and coils of rope, and for hoisting aboard the cod end, full of fish, at the quarters.

Seiners were by now working further afield, and the use of synthetic fibres meant that their fishing gear could be bigger and stronger and could catch more fish, which also called for boats with fuller lines and more deck room and fish carrying capacity.

Star of Peace PD324, delivered from Irvin in 1961, measured 75ft long with beam of 20ft, and had slightly fuller lines than *Silver Hope*, particularly in the forebody, and was beamier and deeper with harder bilges and flatter floors, and was powered by a Gardner 200hp engine. Her original fittings included winch and seine rope coiler fitted forward, Kelvin Hughes echosounder, Decca Navigator, and radio telephone. Seine net skippers relied heavily upon the echosounder, an electronic instrument which indicated the presence of fish shoals and changes in sea bed depth and contour. It was important to be aware of obstructions and rough ground which could easily damage the seine net and ropes, which covered a wide area. Widely used in the fishing fleets, the Decca Navigator was a position finding system which received radio signals from shore-based beacons.

Star of Peace belonged to her original owners, the Baird family, for a long time, and initially worked the seine net but later trawled for herring, sprats, prawns, (*Nephrops norvegicus*), and pink shrimps. In 1994 Skipper John Baird told me 'Irvin's made a bonnie model of a boatie. She has proved her worth sea wise. She's looked after us for thirty three years. If I was in such good condition as the boat is in, I would have no worries.'

Star of Peace was one of nine or ten vessels built to the same hull form. Constructed in 1958 and equipped with Gardner 152hp engine, the white-painted *Fear Not* A249, later PD81, made regular six-day seining trips from Aberdeen under Skipper John Leask, until she was sold to Peterhead owners ten years later.

Built in 1960 for the Duncan family, *Fragrance* PD345 was powered by a Kelvin 240hp motor, and became, in the 1970s, one of the last Scottish boats to work herring drift nets.

Boats became even more substantial. In 1961 Skipper Philip Morgan had *Graceful* PD343 built for seine netting in the more distant waters of the Bergen Bank off Norway in winter, and great-line fishing around the Faroe Islands and Rockall in summer. She measured 78ft 3in with 20ft 6in beam and carried a Gardner 200hp engine. More full bodied than *Star of Peace*, she was four inches deeper with less tuck and flatter floors and harder bilges. Her run was fuller and her cruiser stern more well developed with greater tumblehome, and her stem was raked forward by a further eight inches. Her fish hold had a volume of 3,050 cu ft as against 2,983 for *Star of Peace*.

It was said of *Graceful*, 'She is Irvin's masterpiece; not a kink or a lump anywhere; just a beautiful shape.'

At 78ft long, powered by a Kelvin 240hp motor, and built in 1964, *Glenugie III* PD347 was slightly beamier and deeper than *Graceful*, but was also fuller on the quarter to provide buoyancy for a bigger deckhouse. Delivered in 1966, *Ocean Crest* FR355, later renamed *Hamnavoe* FR345, was in hull form a repeat of *Glenugie III* and also fitted with Kelvin 240hp engine.

Two or three boats were smaller. Measuring 74ft 5in with 20ft 4in beam the seine netter *Prevail* LH444 was handed over in 1966 to Skipper Peter Johnstone and was equipped with a Caterpillar engine which provided a hefty 325 horsepower. Though proportionally slightly fuller in hull form than *Graceful*, she was smaller in order to measure less than fifty gross tons under Scottish Part IV Registry, a calculation based on internal volume. Fishing vessels were subject to regulations which governed their size and manning requirements. Provided a boat fished within certain geographical limits, and did not exceed fifty tons, only the Skipper and not the Second Hand need have a Certificate of Competency.

During a visit to Peterhead in 1994 I found the woebegone remains of *Prevail*. All that survived was part of her bottom structure, looking like some monstrous fungus lying at an oblique angle and decomposing at the edges.

She had perished in the interests of the British government's decommissioning scheme whereby fishermen received payments in order to remove boats from the fleet, but on condition that the vessels be totally destroyed or otherwise permanently disabled. The scheme was designed to meet the European Union's Multiannual Guidance Programme, which called for cuts in boat numbers as a means of conserving fish stocks. *Prevail* was one of forty-six Scottish vessels scheduled for decommissioning at the close of 1993. She was broken up on the site of the Irvin boatyard and so her birthplace became her place of execution. Though the fishermen agreed with curbing over-fishing, they deplored the destruction of so many beautiful boats.

Drifters continued to have a lean time, and Scots were looking at alternative means of herring capture. In 1966, fishing under Skipper Donald Anderson, *Glenugie III* was adapted to work a herring purse seine, which had the catching capacity of ten drifters. The purse seine was set in the form of a huge cylinder around a herring shoal. The net was then closed, or 'pursed', at the bottom so that it resembled a colossal bowl containing the fish. As the netting was hauled, the catch was driven into a diminishing area near the boat and was finally brailed or pumped on board. *Glenugie III*'s success proved the viability of this method of fishing in the Scottish fleet.

2 Capacious

In 1967 Irvin delivered the 82ft by 22ft 3in beam *Vigilant* PD452 to the Buchan family. Fishing under Skipper William Buchan she was the first purse seiner specifically designed and built for the British fleet.

Vigilant embodied many innovations for her builders in terms of design, construction and equipment. Her hull form was developed from that of *Glenugie III*, the lines being opened out to produce a fuller-bodied deeper vessel with gross tonnage of eighty and able to carry large catches. Freeboard was six inches higher, and floors flatter with harder bilges. Frames were double, and some structures such as bulkheads, deck beams and beam stringers were steel for additional strength. Her beam extended well aft to give a roomy buoyant stern for holding the purse seine, which weighed over five tons.

An elderly fisherman was moved to exclaim '… now isn't yon *Vigilant* the finest looking boatie that you ever clapped eyes on …' The fishermen were discerning and knowledgeable critics.

Vigilant had a Caterpillar 410hp engine, and carried powerful hydraulically driven gear handling equipment which included a combined pursing and trawl winch. A power block eliminated the task of hauling the net by hand. Hydraulic rather than mechanical drive was becoming widely accepted in the Scottish fleet. It provided infinitely variable control of deck machinery over a wide range of engine revolutions and allowed freedom to position the equipment where needed.

For herring searching, *Vigilant* carried sonar, which indicated the depth of a shoal and its bearing and distance from the boat and its approximate size and density.

I had a purse seining trip with *Vigilant*, fishing some thirty miles north of the Shetland Islands. My diary recalls that we left Fraserburgh just after midnight '… in a fog. All through the night folks kept singing hymns and songs over the radio telephone. Monday was hot and sunny and sea green and opaque. By evening we were north of Shetland … shot purse net four times for 160 crans. I scrambled about with camera on wheelhouse roof !!! On Tuesday ran down along coast of Shetland—I steered ! ... and we landed at Scalloway in wind and rain.'

This was a small catch. *Vigilant* once caught 797 crans of herring in one cast of her net. A cran amounted to some 3 ½ cwt.

Many fisher folk upheld a strong Christian faith. Their hymn singing was a joy. Fishing crews could form the most exquisite small impromptu choirs.

A particularly favourite hymn was

> Brightly beams our Father's mercy
> From his lighthouse evermore,
> But to us He gives the keeping
> Of the lights along the shore.
> *Philip Bliss, 1838-1876*

Launched early in 1968, Skipper Andrew Strachan's seine netter and herring pair trawler *Achilles* PD178 had satisfying lines and yellow hull. She was quite a favourite and one fisherman said 'There's some would say *Achilles* is perfection.' Pair trawling for herring, in which two boats towed the net between them, was another technique now replacing the drift net. It, too, yielded massive hauls, and required full-bodied, buoyant and strongly constructed powerful boats.

I had a herring trawling trip with *Achilles* some twelve miles off Cape Wrath. We went there through the Pentland Firth which, even in good weather, has an ominous, glutinous, heaving quality like milk about to boil.

At the start of 1969 *Achilles* worked the herring pair trawl in partnership with *Honey Bee* PD110 and *Utilise* PD214, both Irvin-built in the 1950s and originally fitted with Gardner 152hp engines. These had been replaced with Caterpillar 325hp units to provide good pull for the pair trawling. *Honey Bee* was a repeat of *Silver Hope* but one foot shorter, whereas *Utilise* had the same hull form as *Star of Peace*. *Achilles* spent six or seven weeks seine netting in the early summer of 1969 but, during the Shetland herring season, she took some time away from fishing to work as a herring carrier. She joined five other boats transporting herring landed by other vessels in Shetland ports down to Fraserburgh for the kippering and canning factories. Skipper Strachan referred to this herring carrying job as 'fishing for kippers.'

On one occasion I joined *Achilles* in Lerwick and was given a small but important task as part of this herring carrying activity. As each box of fish was swung aboard, I marked it off in a notebook. Laden with herring we ran south to Fraserburgh, passing Fair Isle at sunset.

At 78ft with 22ft beam, *Achilles* was a bit smaller aft than *Vigilant* and had slightly less tuck, but was even fuller forward for carrying big catches. Equipment included Caterpillar 375hp engine and hydraulic seine and trawl winch. In 1970 she was fitted with a power block.

In 1968 Irvin built the 74ft 4in by 20ft 3in beam, 320hp Kelvin-powered seine netter *Stanhope II* PD115 for Skipper Peter Strachan. Meeting the below-fifty-ton criterion she was a slightly deeper version of *Prevail*. Later changing hands, and seine netting under Skipper George Sutherland, she was renamed *Sans Peur* FR212. Both skippers fished her well. Because of this consistently good performance, someone called her 'a good milking cow.' Fishermen are romantics, full of such non-literalities.

Peter Strachan chose the name *Stanhope* on account of the Stanhope Gold Medal he won for rescuing a fellow fisherman.

Introduced in 1873 in memory of the splendidly named naval officer Captain Chandos Scudamore Scudamore Stanhope (1823-1871), the medal is awarded annually by the Royal Humane Society for the greatest act of gallantry during the year. On the night of October 27th, during the 1952 East Anglian herring fishing, the Peterhead drifter *Three Bells* was hauling her nets in deteriorating weather when a rope broke free and threw 59-year old Mate William George Buchan overboard. Eighteen-year old deck hand Peter Strachan jumped in and, with difficulty, swam to windward, reached the 14–15 stone unconscious man and supported him for thirty-five minutes until they could both be hauled back aboard the drifter. Skipper Alex Strachan said 'I consider that in all my sea experience I have never seen nor, in fact, heard of a man being saved in conditions such as prevailed that night.' (Royal Humane Society Annual Report 1952, Case No. 62,839).

Next from Irvin came Skipper Arthur Buchan's *Ugievale II* PD105, with Caterpillar 400hp motor. In shape and size she was similar to *Achilles* but with a slightly finer run, and her stem had a more pronounced forward rake for a more attractive appearance. *Ugievale II* worked with four other Peterhead herring pair trawlers in the team known as the Big Five. Pair trawlers increased their catching and earning capacity with this fleeting system. One pair could be fishing, another brailing her catch aboard, and the others searching for more shoals or heading to port with a full fish hold to catch a favourable market. The Big Five all took part in the searching, fishing and carrying activities and shared their gross earnings equally.

Sailing on board *Ugievale II* I had a trip with the Big Five. We fished off north-east England, 'twixt rivers Tees and Esk, a coastline of dramatic contrasts, with mudflats, marshes and sand dunes and long flat beaches giving way to precipitous high cliffs, and the enchanting river ports of Staithes and Whitby, set at the edge of high, undulating heather moorland. But the chemical and steel working conurbation of Teesside was overhung by a sulphurous miasma visible for miles. We landed our catch in North Shields.

3 Wise Artisanship

My two favourite Irvin boats were the sister ships *Forthright* KY173 and *Steadfast* KY170, built in 1969 for Skippers Robert and Alec Gardner from Anstruther in Fife. Though having similar principal dimensions to *Achilles*, they were even more generously proportioned forward, but were somewhat smaller at the quarters with a finer run, to make them sit in the water better and give them more speed.

For a while, the builders used these two excellent names in their advertisements in the fishing press, although *Forthright* was first to be launched and completed:

STEADFAST AND FORTHRIGHT!

THAT'S IRVIN'S

Many fishing boat names are concerned with volition, the intellect and the exercise of the will. Meaning unswerving and decisive, the name *Forthright* might seem appropriate, but it had a significance beyond the obvious. Skipper Robert Gardner said that he wanted a name containing 'Forth', as in the Firth of Forth.

When seen alongside *Forthright* and *Steadfast*, the earlier boats such as *Silver Hope* and *Star of Peace* looked lean and spare, restrained and finely drawn. At her skipper's request *Forthright* was given a slightly more pronounced sheer forward than *Steadfast* to give a more graceful appearance.

Each was powered by a Caterpillar six-cylinder 400hp and 1,225rpm engine which turned a 66in-diameter fixed-pitch propeller through a 4.09:1 reverse and reduction gearbox. Large slow-turning propellers gave good pulling power for working trawls and seine nets. Marine motors in which the crankshaft rotated at a medium number of revolutions per minute were chosen for their lighter weight and compact size in relation to lower-reving units. But large reduction gears were necessary to provide the required lower propeller speeds.

I first met *Forthright* and *Steadfast* when they were under construction. Occasionally everything disappeared in purple fog. This was caused by the welding being done on *Forthright*'s steel beams casting a purplish brilliant light onto clouds of steam. The steam came from the box in which *Steadfast*'s planks were being steamed to make them supple and bendable for fastening to the frames. When their hulls were complete, they were launched, and then fitted out alongside the quay. *Forthright* went down the slipway quickly. A crew member later told me 'We knew she would do well because she made a big splash and broke the ropes when she was launched, and went careering right across the harbour; eager to be off, ye ken.'

I asked if she was a good sea boat, and was told 'Yon's such a great lump of a boatie, she couldn't be much else.'

Apart from making a few herring trawling trips off the Scottish west coast, *Forthright* and *Steadfast* concentrated on flydragging seine net fishing, undertaking trips of less than a week to grounds such as the Bergen Bank some 200 miles north-east of Aberdeen. Seine netting was a tiring job. A crewman on board *Forthright* said he had once been gutting fish while he was asleep.

Catches consisted largely of haddock and cod which were packed in ice in seven stone wooden boxes, and landings were normally made in Aberdeen but sometimes in Peterhead or North Shields. They were very much sisters, as they often fished in proximity and put ashore their catches on the same day. During the early 1970s they were among the highest earning Scottish seiners and were known for landing high quality fish nicely presented for auction and in keen demand from the buyers.

Following Scottish practice, the hulls of *Forthright* and *Steadfast* were built of larch planking on an oak framework, with an Oregon pine deck. Oak is tough and durable and can be obtained with a natural sweep of grain from which to cut curved components such as frames. Available in long lengths, larch is straight grained and abrasion resistant. Oregon pine is close grained and strong and mostly knot-free.

The two boats had similar fittings. On deck a hydraulically powered combined seine and trawl winch and a 'Beccles' rope coiler were positioned forward. A power block was fitted abaft the deckhouse. Wheelhouse instruments included radar, radio telephone, fish-finding echo sounders, Decca Navigator and automatic pilot. Mess deck and galley with gas cooker were positioned abaft the wheelhouse.

I once cooked breakfast for eight on board *Steadfast* after she had put ashore her catch in Aberdeen. Such meals on the fishing boats were stupendous; great early morning helpings of bacon, eggs, tomatoes, sausages, black pudding, fried bread and fried bananas and plenteous fulsome galley tea with condensed milk…

Forthright was still fishing from Aberdeen in the early 1990s, but was later decommissioned and broken up. *Steadfast* sank in 1982 following a collision with an oil rig tender on the Ekofisk oil field . Her crew were picked up by the tender.

During the late 1960s I spent much time in the Irvin shed.

Designer and loftsman George McKechnie showed me how variations in boat shape were achieved. He often spoke about his ways of doing things, his philosophy that even good designs were worth further investigation and change and development. I was spellbound by the way he weighed up problems and found a solution.

'*Prevail* drops her head a bit. Maybe she's too fine in the bilge. I'll give *Stanhope* lower bilges and flatter floors.'

'I thought perhaps I'd make *Stanhope*'s stem longer but maybe I'll leave it as it is.'

Years later, a prominent naval architect told me that George McKechnie had known exactly what to do. Though not knowing the scientific theory of vessel design, George had got it 'just right.' George spoke highly of Mr J. E. Smith, designer at the time of building *Silver Hope*. 'Mr Smith now, he would talk for hours about boats; in fact Mr Smith *was* boats.'

A lines drawing delineates a boat's solid curvilinear form on a sheet of paper. Existing drawings could be modified in order to determine changes in the shape of consecutive vessels. There was much discussion between designer and skipper, and the drawings were a splendid means of comparing such complex hull forms and their subtle interrelationships and variables. It was customary to make a scale half-model in order to assess the eyesweet quality of the shape and detect any inconsistencies, which could then be corrected in a final lines drawing. A general arrangement plan was also prepared, showing the position of principal fittings such as engine, winches and superstructure.

When drawn full size on the floor of the mould loft, in the process known as lofting, the lines and any other necessary information enabled all measurements to be taken, and templates, or 'moulds,' created for building the hull of the boat. Irvin's lofting procedure was standard practice at that time.

It was a complex process, needing great care and careful checking, or 'fairing', to ensure that all three sets of curves, in plan and side and end elevations, were in accordance with one another. Many calculations were made at the lofting stage, including the amount of bevel required on the frames to enable the planks to fit. I was intrigued by the whole thing. Others were fascinated too. George said 'I usually lock the loft door at lunchtime because the fishermen go in and walk all over the lines.'

Sometimes existing moulds were adjusted to produce alterations in hull form. Extra pieces were added to *Prevail*'s moulds which were then used for shaping the framework of *Stanhope II* to provide her with greater buoyancy where needed.

George said that some boats 'came naturally' at the lines drawings and lofting stages, just developed nicely under his hands. But he had to fight his way along with others. He had the mind-set of the true artist, who may struggle with a painting but finally produces something of great quality.

4 Remarkable Run of Affairs

Forthright and *Steadfast* were exceptionally full-lined boats for their time, particularly in the forebody. There were those who thought them too buxom.

Skipper John C. Buchan wanted his 79.20ft seiner and herring pair trawler *Sparkling Star* PD108, built in 1970, to be finer forward and aft, with more tuck and a finer underbody so that she would not need so much ballast. She was 22ft 3in on the beam, with gross tonnage of seventy-six, but her run was even finer than that of *Graceful*. Continuing the trend towards higher power, she had a Lister Blackstone six cylinder motor providing 495hp. *Sparkling Star* was a member of the Big Five herring trawling team.

Under Skipper John Scally, the slightly smaller *Enterprise* FR64 joined the Fraserburgh fleet later the same year. A sweet-lined craft measuring 75ft 8in with 20ft 6in beam she was similar in hull shape to *Stanhope II* but slightly longer and beamier with gross tonnage of fifty-nine and powered by a Caterpillar 425hp engine.

But there was a tragedy. Though known as an excellent sea boat which withstood adverse weather, *Enterprise* was lost at sea with all hands. She was last heard from on February 23rd in 1978, some ninety miles east of Sumburgh Head in the Shetland Islands, in winds increasing to force ten. Scots were deeply unsettled by a number of vessel disappearances during that decade.

Sometime about 1971 I became Scotland Correspondent for *Fishing News*. Founded in Aberdeen in 1913 and later moving to London, this weekly journal published news and feature articles on all aspects of the commercial fishing industry. I was given freedom to develop my particular specialities and I photographed and wrote about the new boats with enthusiasm. Fishing and boatbuilding people were always helpful, kindly, supportive and informative. Perhaps I was accepted as part of the fabric of the harbours.

And, in a series of monthly reports, I described the remarkable run of affairs in Peterhead. From being a failed and bedraggled herring centre in the 1960s, with weeds growing on the quaysides, Peterhead became in the 1980s the principal British fishing port for the weight and value of catches brought ashore. This awe-inspiring rise to prominence began in 1970 when many seine net skippers boycotted Aberdeen in protest against high landing expenses in that grey granite city.

But the developments also reflected shortfalls elsewhere. During the 1970s, loss of access to traditional distant water fishing grounds such as Iceland led to the rapid decline of the once prosperous English deep sea trawling ports of Hull and Grimsby, and also affected Aberdeen.

Peterhead built up a mighty infrastructure, with major harbour and fish market improvements and, by 1980, almost 400 boats and 2,700 fishermen worked from the port, catching demersal fish, predominantly haddock, cod and whiting.

Whereas a vast fleet of some 300 seine netters provided some eighty per cent of the catch in the late 1970s, there was a move to pair trawling for demersal species which enabled the boats to work over rockier ground. In 1981 more than forty pair trawling partnerships put up a tremendous performance landing vast quantities of cod and coalfish.

Situated on an east-facing craggy promontory north of Aberdeen, and built of local pink granite, Peterhead often seems bleak and desolate in swirling fogs and sleety winter storms, but in summer it sparkles in a brilliant but cool northern light under some of the clearest skies in Europe, and the sea becomes a translucent jade green.

Politically and economically the 1970s were peculiar years, with harmful phases of uncertainty, alarm and downturn. Sometimes the profitability of the fleet was lowered by cheap imports of foreign fish and a savage rise in fuel costs. But stocks of cod and other species were high, and a growing awareness of the nutritional value of fish often pushed quayside prices above all previous expectations, and the fisheries prospered enormously.

Fishermen wanted capable boats, able to work new catching techniques to advantage. Boatyards were inundated with orders. Vessel design was changing. Introduced in the 1960s, the transom stern marked a radical departure in Scottish wooden hulled boats, in that the hull abaft the stern post ended square and provided more width and space aft. Onwards from 1969 there was also a huge demand for steel craft in the 40ft to 90ft size range. But the cruiser stern was still preferred by many seine net skippers because its rounded shape provided a smooth and continuous support for the incoming ropes. Some thought it gave a boat superior handling qualities.

Among builders of wooden vessels who were still active at the time, Irvin never did build a transom-sterned boat. Each builder had its own particular style, which the fishermen could recognise. They said that the archetypal Scottish cruiser-sterned vessels rarely shipped lumps of green water over the side or stern, and functioned equally well running before the seas or heading into them. Normally they had a high 'GM', or metacentric height, a characteristic which caused them to recover quickly and strongly from a roll, and was a good stability feature. In the 1970s, when new safety regulations stipulated that the stability of existing boats be assessed, the majority of Scottish seiner trawlers were found to be above the minimum requirements.

Starting in 1971, Irvin built ten boats upwards of 79ft long and seventy-eight gross tons, all bigger than *Forthright* and *Steadfast* and with roomier sterns. In addition it produced the 72ft 3in *Sunbeam* INS74 at just short of fifty tons. All were pleasing to the eye and hugely admired. Equipped to work seine nets and single or pair trawls, they were among the largest of their type to join the Scottish fleets during that decade.

Good looking 79.9ft and 22ft 6in beam *Reliant* BCK36 was handed over to Skipper John Addison in 1971 and joined the large fleet of seine netters already fishing from Peterhead. Her Kelvin engine produced 400hp at 1,150rpm to turn the propeller through a 4:1 reduction gearbox. On deck *Reliant* carried a fish gutting machine which relieved crewmen from the arduous task of gutting much of the catch by hand. In common with several Scottish boatyards, Irvin used sub contactors for much fitting-out work, including machinery installation, and the fabrication of deck houses and other steel structures. *Reliant*'s main and auxiliary engines and her winch were installed by a new Peterhead company headed by marine engineer James Wiseman.

In 1970, fifty-five per cent of the total British herring catch was landed by trawlers, compared with only eighteen per cent in 1966, and the Scottish pair trawling partnerships were highly efficacious. But the Scots were striving to perfect the technique even further, and were building even more useful boats with greater catching power and net towing strength. Nets were becoming larger and more complex in design and could handle massive hauls.

Skipper George Collin was one of the most successful of all herring fishermen, and his 79ft by 22ft 6in *Star Crest* PD114, delivered from Irvin in 1971, was equipped primarily as a herring pair trawler. Her Caterpillar 565hp motor was, at that time, the most powerful to be installed in a Scottish wooden-hulled vessel. A special towing post, on the centreline abaft her deckhouse, gave her better manoeuvrability and towing efficiency.

Her net was even bigger than normal. It was considered that larger, slower moving nets, with bigger meshes at their forward end, could cause less turbulence. Thus the herring shoals were less likely to react and scatter. To achieve even greater trawling accuracy, *Star Crest* carried a net sounder. A transducer on the headline transmitted echoes to an echo sounder in the wheelhouse, and enabled the height of the net opening to be judged.

Herring catching in Scotland in the early 1970s was concentrated chiefly in the Minches, part of the inner seas off the west coast. *Star Crest* and her three partner vessels enjoyed a lucrative fishing. Just before Christmas 1973, five hundred crans were caught in *Star Crest*'s net, said to be the largest catch taken in a single tow by a Scottish pair trawler that winter. Early the following year, in abnormally bad weather, I saw *Star Crest* unloading herring in Mallaig. Set among wild terrain, this small, isolated, West Highland village was, for a short time, the leading herring port in Europe, with more than a hundred boats working an area from south of Barra Head to the north end of South Uist.

Peterhead meanwhile was firmly established as the main demersal port in Scotland after Aberdeen, with the value of landings in 1972 being double the 1971 figure.

Irvin kept busy.

Equipped primarily for seine net fishing, the robust eighty-footers *Ulysses* PD76 and *Achieve* FR100 were delivered in 1972 to Skippers Andrew Reid and Andrew Buchan. With 22.75ft beam and gross tonnage of just above eighty they were powered by Caterpillar engines giving 565hp and 450hp respectively.

Demand for fish was high, and skippers were confident in the future of their fisheries. Lossiemouth skipper William Smith took command of the forty-nine gross tons, 72ft 3in by 20ft 2in beam *Sunbeam* INS74, completed early in 1973 and fitted with Caterpillar 380hp motor.

In 1973 more than twenty-five vessels were under construction or on order for Peterhead, in British and Continental boatyards. Capacious and doughty eighty-four-footer *Resplendent* PD38 was handed over from Irvin in 1973 to seine net specialist

Skipper David John Forman. Her broad 23ft 6in beam, 91.20 gross tonnage, and her low hard bilges gave her exceptionally large internal space, and enabled her to carry 900 boxes of fish. She landed 650 boxes from her maiden trip. The Mirrlees Blackstone 495hp, 750rpm motor drove the propeller through a 2.5:1 reduction gearbox. Slower revving engines do not require such large reduction gears in order to achieve suitable propeller speeds, and though heavier and larger they were suitable for these bigger vessels. There were new ideas for handling seine net ropes. On board *Resplendent* storage bins were arranged at the forward end of her fishroom, and the ropes travelled down from the coiler via hatches in the deck.

Irvin normally built two boats at a time. *Graceful* PD133 ran her trials on June 25th in 1974, and *Daisy* PD123 was completed a few weeks later. Both 79ft 6in long and 22ft 8in on the beam, and built respectively for Skippers Philip Morgan and James Bruce, they had different principal fittings. *Graceful* was powered by a Mirrlees Blackstone 495hp, 750rpm engine with 2.5:1 reduction gearbox. *Daisy*'s Grenaa 550hp motor ran at 500rpm and therefore did not need a reduction gearbox. Her controllable pitch propeller, as opposed to the usual fixed pitch type, gave more efficient use of engine power according to whether she was fishing or running free.

Safety of vessels and crewmen was coming to the forefront. *Daisy* was among the first half dozen Scottish boats to have seine rope storage reels. These eliminated the dangerous tasks of arranging coils of rope on deck when the gear was being hauled, and later standing near them to ensure that they ran out smoothly.

Boats were often named after flowers, conjuring up images of something delicate, quiet, tranquil, safe and sweet, and in a non-nautical setting. This is much at variance with the boats themselves, which were stalwart, tarry and water-borne, amid spume and storms, salt-caked and bespattered with opalescent fish scales, and emitting diesel vapours.

Perhaps the art of choosing a name for a boat can be seen as the creation of a one or two-word poem, creating word association, the linking of ideas, and the use of metaphor and symbolism and word-play.

5   Heady Days

The fishing industry is rich in things quirky and idiosyncratic.

Sometime around 1970 I took a photograph of boat names chalked on a wall in the Irvin mould loft.

Today the image is held in public and private collections including London's Tate Britain, and the University of Indiana. It was published by internationally known poet and artist Ian Hamilton Finlay in the form of a postcard, to which he had given the title *A Sea Street Anthology*. It was, he explained, 'as if the boats were living things and had chalked their names on the wall of the street where they lived.'

Finlay (1925-2006) made an important contribution to modern linguistic philosophy, and used fishing boat names as a point of departure for much of his work. His experimental poems, sometimes only one or two words long, were published in limited editions, elegantly designed and printed in the form of booklets, postcards, and prints, which were issued by his own Wild Hawthorn Press. He was concerned with a bringing together of words and images which were full of verbal and visual puns and metaphors and word-play, and complex layers of meaning, sometimes haunting, contemplative, and deeply philosophical. Often he worked with collaborators, well regarded artists and designers who produced visual images through which Ian conveyed his ideas. These collaborative relationships were key to his way of doing things. He set out to broaden the limits of poetry, and to extend our interpretation of the written word. Sometimes he created 'found poems', which take existing texts from other sources and impart to them new and profound meanings by adding further words. I was one of Ian's collaborators. My photograph was a 'found text' which appealed to him in many ways. He said that he was interested in the comings and goings of the boats. They have life stories; things happen to them. Fishermen say that their vessels develop personality and character and individual modes of behaviour.

One of Finlay's aims was to encourage us to contemplate his work, create our own threads of thought, take them further and build new definitions and considerations.

People in the fishing and boatbuilding communities would remember one or more of these boats in their own way. For me, the list is elegiac, a lament for a lost time, sometimes melancholy but celebratory too. Here and there the list is haphazard. Several boats are not recorded in their order of building. Why had the names been written there? Most of the vessels are now gone but are held in long remembrance.

Perhaps the chalked list can be looked upon as a fine example of graffiti, in the way that names are scribbled in public places to record a person's presence at a particular moment. Such marks can survive for years, and can offer a glimpse into matters historical.

Graffiti is now regarded as street art, very much part of popular culture and a powerful means of expression. All these boats had been in the Irvin shed. It was where they had come into being.

Replenish FR199, delivered to Skipper James Green in 1975, was the hundredth vessel built by Irvin. At 80ft with 22ft 8in beam she carried a Mirrlees Blackstone 495hp engine with reduction gearbox and controllable pitch propeller. Seine ropes were stored in bins.

There were setbacks. Completion of Skipper William Stephen's 79ft 6in and 22ft 8in beam *Radiant Way* FR191 early in 1976 left the Irvin order book empty. Another recession in mid-decade had caused a fall-off in new boat building. In the end, the despondency lifted, and the value of fish landed by British vessels at Scottish ports rose from £59.3 million in 1975 to a colossal £85.8 million in 1976 and, as the rate of inflation began to ease down the boats enjoyed an increase in their real income.

Radiant Way had a particularly powerful Caterpillar 725hp 1800rpm engine and controllable pitch propeller and 5.4:1 reduction ratio.

In 1975 about forty-five Irvin-built boats were still fishing from Scottish ports, some ageing but not going to seed. One such was Skipper George Baird's 73ft seine netter *Duncairn* PD477, completed in 1954 as *Trustful II* PD477, with beam of 19ft 6in and a repeat in hull form of *Silver Hope*. Though still somewhat steep, her running costs were less than those of a new vessel. During 1975 the fleet's expenses had risen by some twenty-five per cent compared to the previous year. In 1975 a crewman told me that *Duncairn*'s Gardner 152hp engine was 'running like new'. She had just landed 353 boxes of fish, which was quite a decent catch for that time.

My photograph of *Duncairn* and drawing of *Daisy* show their quite remarkable differences in hull shape and deckhouse design. *Duncairn* would not initially have a power block, and probably no whaleback.

A handful of Irvin boats found themselves elsewhere. In the middle of the 1976 heatwave I visited former Peterhead vessel *Constant Friend* PD131 in the Devon port of Brixham. Working flydragging seine nets under Skipper Tony Rae, she sometimes fished fifteen to twenty miles south of the Eddystone lighthouse and caught valuable lemon soles and red mullet.

Fishing with seine nets in the English Channel was hazardous. Nets could snag on huge amounts of debris from two World Wars. But top quality catches were definitely the main asset of the seine net. Sister ship to *Silver Hope*, *Constant Friend* was built in the 1950s, and in 1976 was the only seiner working from Brixham.

Irvin did not only build these bigger boats. They had, since World War II, produced some twenty seine netters chiefly 60ft to 66ft long, for the Moray Firth ports of Buckie and Lossiemouth. There were two small notable exceptions, one being little 39.8ft *Golden View* PD184, produced in the 1950s for Peterhead. Boats not more than 40ft long could legally catch demersal fish with seine nets, within certain areas in Aberdeenshire waters between sunrise and sunset.

Following the completion of *Radiant Way* it was thought that Irvin might build no more boats, but in 1978 they delivered *Sunbeam* INS189 to Skipper William Smith. At 85ft with 24ft beam she was the final over-76ft wooden hulled cruiser sterned vessel built in Scotland. *Sunbeam* was powered by a 600hp, 750rpm Mirrlees Blackstone engine with 3:1 reduction gearbox and fixed pitch propeller, and carried rope storage reels. Robust cantilever trawl gallows, built into the after end of her deckhouse, carried towing blocks for single and pair trawling. An aluminium deck shelter was arranged around the forward end of her deckhouse. Introduced into the Scottish seiner trawler fleet in the early 1970s, such structures were becoming standard fittings.

Fishing boat design was becoming more formalised. *Sunbeam* satisfied *The Fishing Vessels (Safety Provisions) Rules 1975* which laid down statutory requirements in respect of many factors including stability, freeboard and hull strength. Independent firms of naval architects collaborated with builders to fulfil these stipulations. Stability describes the ability of a boat to come upright after being heeled over by an outside force. Preliminary stability assessment could be carried out at the early design stage.

Stability calculations for *Sunbeam* were handled by the Napier Company (Arbroath) Ltd., which was a well-known authority on the subject.

Sunbeam fared well at the seine net. More and more boats were cramming into Peterhead. On June 15th 1979 an extension to the fish market came into use for the first time when *Sunbeam* landed a 670-box seine net catch. To mark the occasion, the first box of fish was sold for £88 which was donated to the Royal National Mission to Deep Sea Fishermen. *Sunbeam* made a tremendous start to 1980, setting up a Scottish earnings record for a single trip by a seiner, with 1,104 boxes of fish worth £27,119, landed at Peterhead after only two days' fishing. This was also a port record for the weight of fish put ashore by a seiner from only one outing.

These were heady and successful days. Although vessel decommissioning programmes were yet to come, and the European Community's Common Fisheries Policy, with its catch quota regime, was not introduced until 1983, fishermen were aware of the dangers of over fishing. Already there were some catch restrictions on those species considered to be under serious pressure, and in fact the main herring fisheries around the British Isles were closed for several years.

At the time of *Sunbeam*'s completion, Irvin had new ideas. They hoped to build timber-hulled vessels 54ft to 86ft long, but also to fit out steel boats, the hulls of which would be built elsewhere. But this was not to happen, and *Sunbeam* was the yard's final boat.

The Irvin boatbuilding business was founded in 1914 when fishing company Richard Irvin & Sons Ltd acquired Peterhead builder of steam powered herring drifters Forbes & Birnie.

Registered in North Shields in 1871, Irvin had wide interests in the fishing and maritime industries, and became a well-known firm of fishing vessel owners and managers, fish salesmen and chandlers, with branches in many ports.

For much of the twentieth century the company operated deep sea trawlers from North Shields and Aberdeen. Many were named after hills and mountains with the prefix *Ben*, and are fondly recalled as the 'ben' boats. Trawler owning firms normally used a particular theme for naming their vessels.

Initially at Peterhead Irvin built two or three steam drifters for its own fleet, and then concentrated on repair work until in 1937 it delivered the 65ft cruiser-sterned motor boat *Valkyrie* II to Fraserburgh. During World War II Irvin produced vessels for the defence fleet, including motor minesweepers 105ft long, and also 75ft cruiser sterned Motor Fishing Vessels which were used for many wartime duties.

Following the close of hostilities the firm concentrated on the cruiser-sterned fishing boats, starting in the mid-1940s with *Rambler Rose* BF104 at 66ft 3in with 18ft beam, and powered by a Gleniffer 160hp diesel engine.

Illustrations

1. Designed as a herring drifter and great-line boat, *Silver Hope* was elegant and lissom and clean-lined.

2. *Silver Hope* is on the slipway in Peterhead for a repaint. In Scotland, the concavity in her underbody is known as tuck, but it has otherwise been described as hollow garboards, or hollow floors.

3. *Star of Peace* sets out from Peterhead in the 1960s for a seine netting trip. Irvin's premises are astern of her.

4. Skipper John Baird said that *Star of Peace* attracted attention in any port she visited.

5. *Star of Peace* lies on the slipway for a much needed repaint. Her modest cruiser stern can be seen to advantage here.

6. Lovely 75-footer *Fear Not* gets under way from Peterhead in the 1960s, during one of my earliest visits to the fishertown.

7. Much admired *Fear Not* takes on ice in Peterhead. A white painted hull was uncustomary in Scotland.

8. *Fragrance* has just landed a seine net trip in Aberdeen. In 1968 she was the only Peterhead boat to work the herring drift nets, whereas more than a hundred steam powered drifters were registered at the port before the Second World War.

9. *Fragrance* changed hands and was renamed **_Westward_**.
She spent time trawling for prawns whose scientific name is *Nephrops norvegicus*.
These are a valuable shellfish species and the tails are marketed as scampi.

10. *Graceful*'s lines were more filled out than those of *Star of Peace* and she was beamier and deeper.

11. *Glenugie III* achieved greatness. Fishing under Skipper Donald Anderson in 1966, she began the mighty Scottish herring purse seine fishery. Later she returned to flydragging seine netting for demersal species when larger purse seiners became necessary.

12. *Hamnavoe*, originally *Ocean Crest* FR355, was under construction in 1965 when I first visited the Irvin shed.

13. *Ocean Crest* lands herring in Aberdeen in 1970 following a drift netting trip. This fishing method was in steep decline.

14. *Prevail* puts ashore a seine net catch in Peterhead.
At other times she landed in North Shields and Aberdeen.

15. *Prevail* looks glossy and refreshed after a repaint. Note the figures and the small boat alongside her. There is always something pleasing going on around the harbours.

16. The decommissioning schemes caused huge distress.
Prevail was broken up on the site of the Irvin boatyard, which was an unkindly twist of fate.

17. *Vigilant* was the first boat designed and built for the British herring purse seine fleet.

18. In general appearance *Vigilant* was akin to the traditional Scottish cruiser sterned beauties, but was chunkier and more heavily constructed to handle the purse seine and huge herring hauls.

19. I had a herring purse seining trip with *Vigilant*.
Here, crewmembers guide the netting as it is being hauled on board through the power block.

20. Herring is lifted out of *Vigilant*'s purse seine by means of a brailer net.

21. Crewmen on board *Vigilant* repair the purse seine.

22. *Achilles* was the favourite of many.
Note the coils of seine net rope forward, and the power block abaft the deckhouse. The ice making factory in Peterhead was a marvellous place from which to look at the boats.

23. *Achilles* starts out for the seine netting. Her full forward lines are very noticeable here. The nearest boat in the group of three is *Adoration* PD207, built by Irvin in 1957 and similar in shape to *Star of Peace*.

24. A net is sorted alongside *Achilles*. She originally carried a mizzen sail.

25. *Utilise* leaves Peterhead for the seine net grounds.
Later she worked the herring pair trawl in partnership with *Achilles* and *Honey Bee*.

26. Early in 1968 ***Stanhope II***, in the foreground, and ***Ugievale II*** are under construction. A cloud of steam is about to befog the shed. This comes from the steam box in which *Stanhope II*'s planks are being made pliable.

27. *Stanhope II* has just landed a seine net trip in Aberdeen. She took her name from the Stanhope Gold Medal which Skipper Peter Strachan won for saving the life of a fellow fisherman.

28. Slipways were good places on which to contemplate boat shape. ***Stanhope II*** was of slighter form than *Ugievale II*.

29. All the Irvin boats were in high favour, to everyone's liking. *Stanhope II*'s pleasing lines can be appreciated here.

30. Boats were now more robustly constructed than hitherto. Here, *Ugievale II* is in frame.

31. *Ugievale II* was among the first to be built with pair trawling in mind. When two boats towed the net between them, herring, mackerel, cod and coalfish were caught in large quantities.

32. Sister ships *Forthright* and *Steadfast* are being fitted out. Their skippers belonged to Anstruther in Fife, and so the boats were registered at Kirkcaldy.

33. *Forthright* was immoderately full bodied forward, but her lines fined away a bit towards the stern.

34. Famed as being one of the highest earning flydragging seine netters in the United Kingdom, *Forthright* sets out from Peterhead.

35. Early in 1971 *Forthright* makes a brief foray into herring pair trawling from Mallaig on the Scottish west coast, working in partnership with *Steadfast* and three other vessels.

36. In comparison to *Silver Hope*, (photos 1 & 2), **Forthright** is beamier, with much fuller forward lines, and less tuck.

37. In 1973, in Peterhead, *Forthright* puts ashore 820 boxes of fish, thought at the time to be the biggest amount caught by a flydragging seiner in one trip. A good layer of ice covers the fish to maintain quality. She was now fishing under Skipper George Hodge.

38. A final few fish from *Forthright*'s big catch are swung ashore. A basket is used because all her boxes have already been filled.

39. *Steadfast* is launched on July 1st 1969 at about a quarter to three on a hot sunny afternoon. It was standard practice at Irvin to fit out the boats after their hulls had been put in the water.

40. *Steadfast* has just landed a seine net catch in Aberdeen, and is pulling away from the quayside. Her deckhouse was of different shape to that of Forthright.

41. Early in 1971, *Steadfast* lies on the Peterhead slipway for a repaint, most probably after her return from the herring pair trawling.

42. Sometime around 1975 *Steadfast* was fitted with a deck shelter, arranged around the forward end of her deckhouse. Such structures became standard fittings on the seine netters.

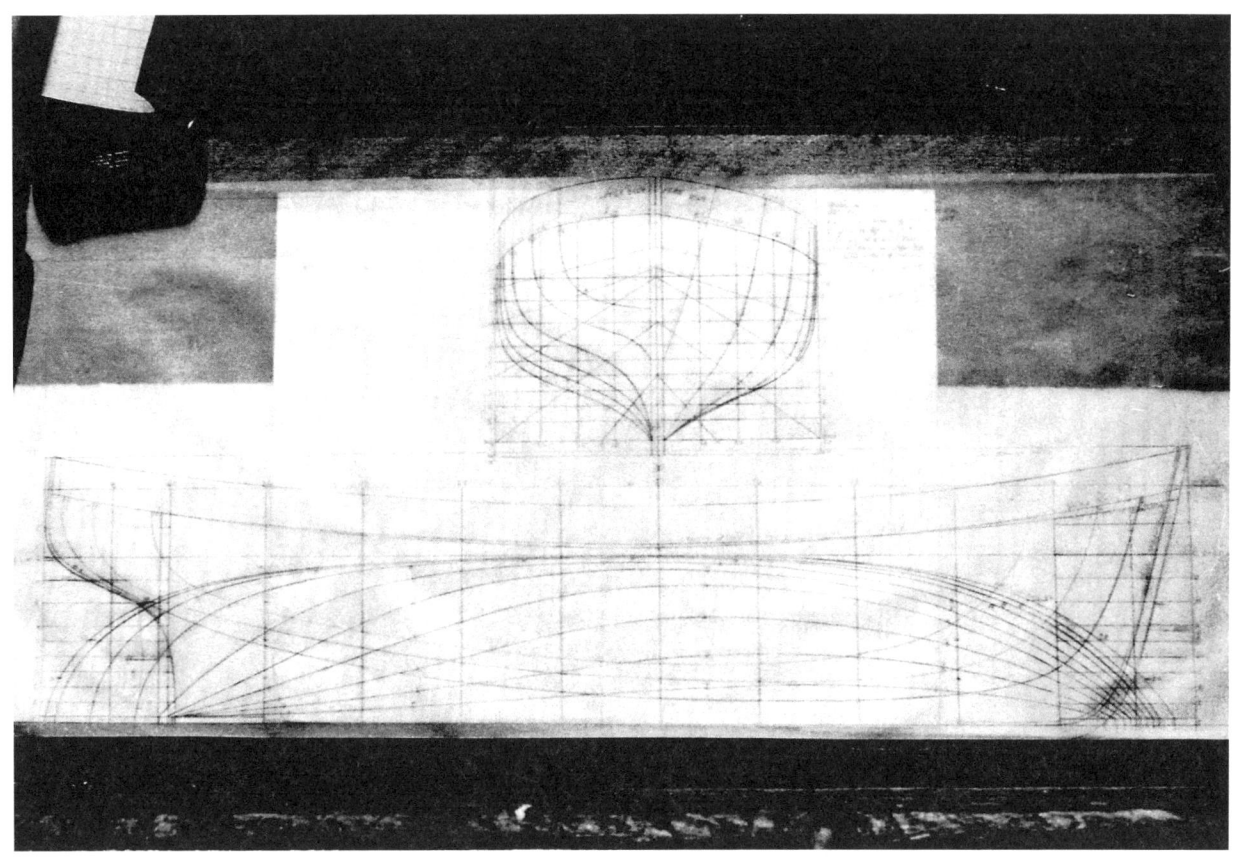

43. These lines drawings for *Forthright* and *Steadfast* describe their hull form from three salient angles. They were then drawn full size on the mould loft floor.

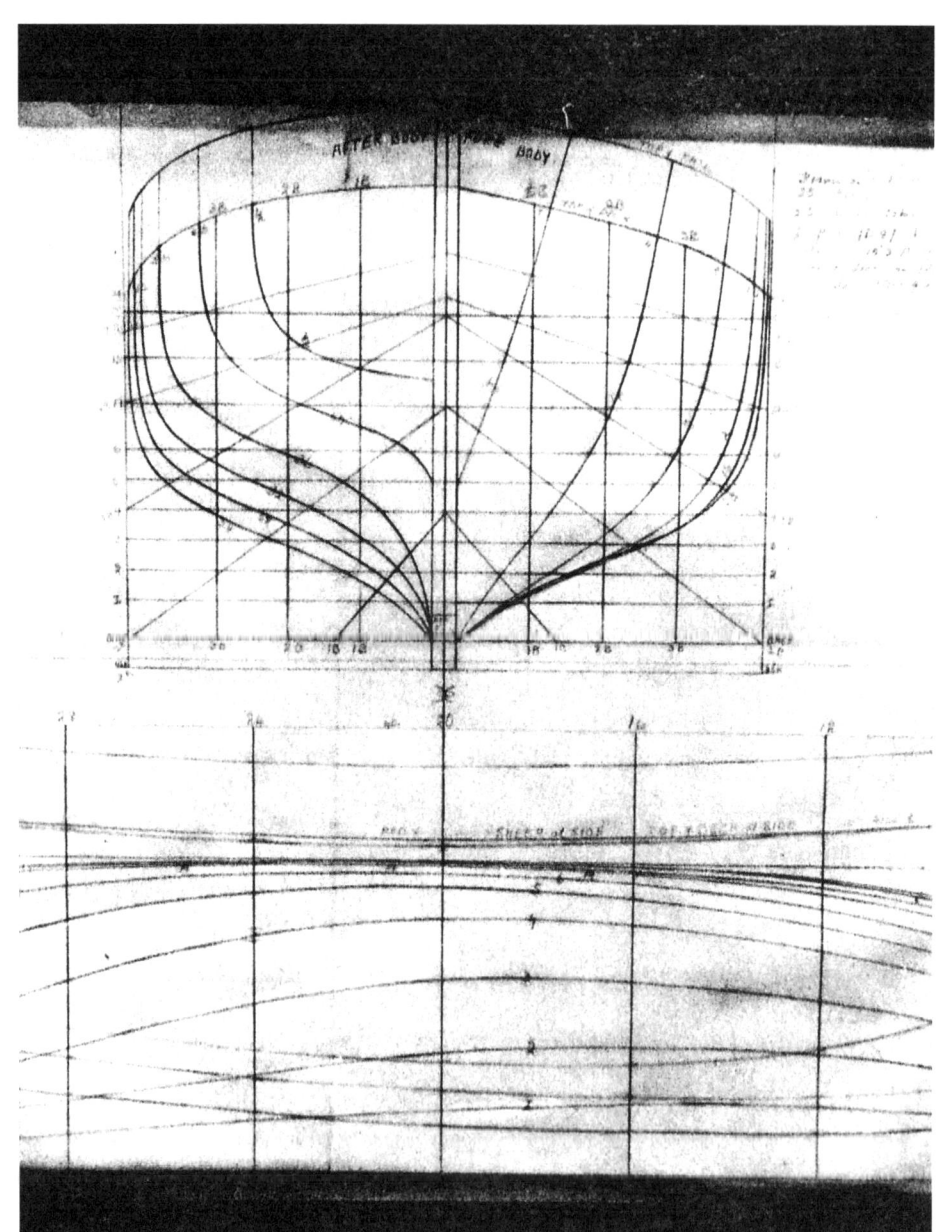

44. Lines drawings describe the hull shape. This body plan for ***Forthright*** and ***Steadfast*** shows their plump bow form. Their tuck was less pronounced than that of *Silver Hope* (photos 1 & 2).

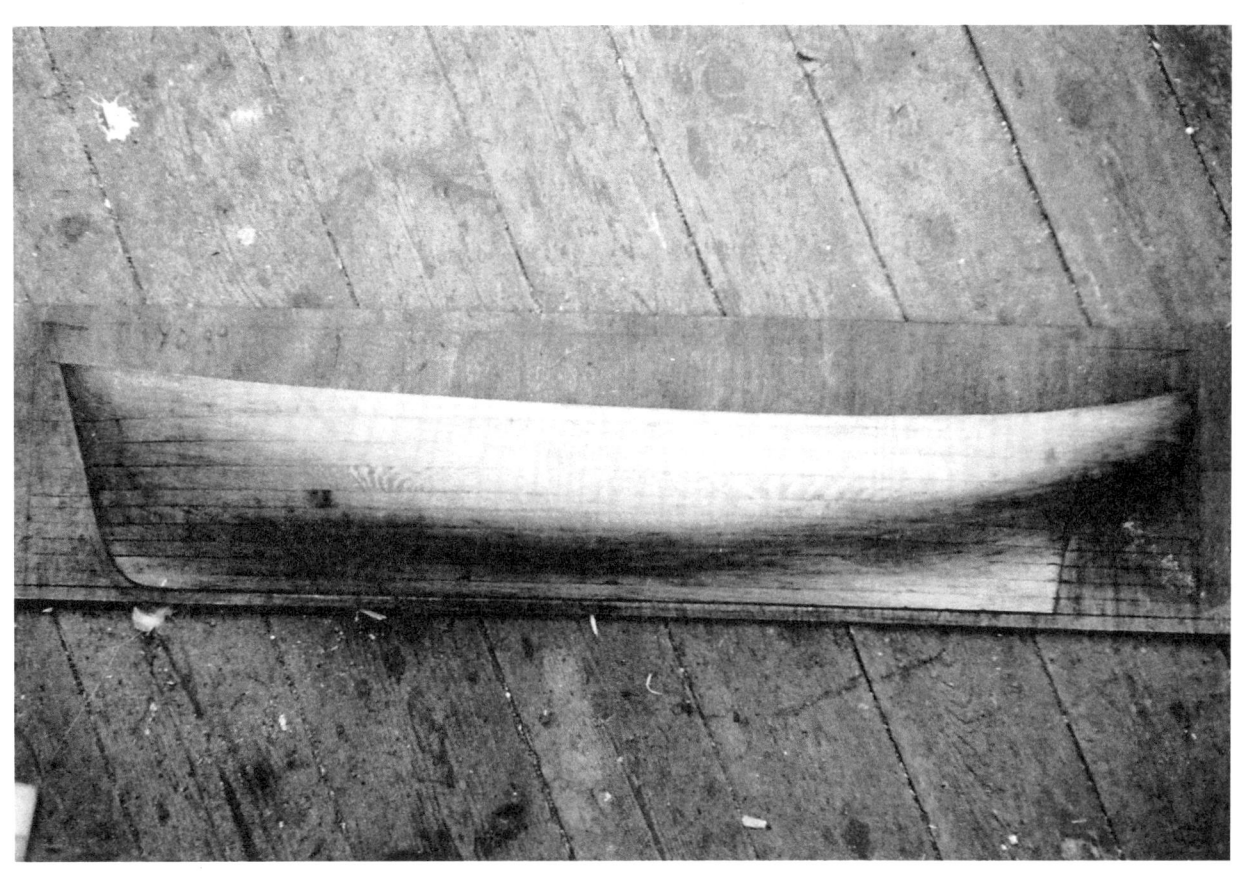

45. A half-model is made as part of the design process.
Great care is necessary, to ensure that it corresponds with the lines drawings in shape.

46. George McKechnie, kneeling, works on the process known as lofting, in which a boat's lines are drawn full scale. This is the body plan for *Sparkling Star*, built in 1970.

47. Much measuring and checking is required to ensure that the lines on the floor agree in all three projections.

48. This is one of the moulds , or templates, which were used for shaping the frames of *Sparkling Star*.

49. Extra pieces were added to the bottom of *Prevail*'s moulds, which were then used for shaping the frames of **Stanhope II** to provide greater buoyancy. So *Stanhope II*'s bilges were lower and floors flatter, as can be seen in the mould in the left foreground.

50. I kept notebooks. Though by no means accurate, this sketch illustrates my exploration of the relative hull shapes of *Achilles* and *Forthright* and *Steadfast*. It shows, nevertheless, that the latter two were fuller forward than *Achilles*, and finer at the quarters.

51. Despite being of similar length and beam to *Forthright* and *Steadfast*, *Sparkling Star* was more modest in shape, without the exceptionally full forebody.

52. *Sparkling Star* spent much of her time at the herring pair trawling but also worked flydragging seine nets.

53. Seen from *Ugievale II*, **Sparkling Star** searches for herring off the North Yorkshire coast.

54. (a, b, c) In the 1970s there were several Scottish fishing tragedies. ***Enterprise*** was lost at sea, sadly with all hands.

55. There were extraordinary scenes in **Peterhead** in 1970 when hundreds of boxes of fish were laid out for auction in the open air upon every available quay space. Seine netters had boycotted Aberdeen in protest against high charges for landing their catches there.

56. Two or three Irvin-built boats are among this group *c*1970 in **Peterhead**. *Stanhope II* PD115 is on the far right, and the recently completed *Sparkling Star* PD108 lies stern outwards, second from left. Lying to starboard of *Sparkling Star* is *Adoration* PD207, built in the 1950s and similar in hull form to *Star of Peace*.

57. The boycott of Aberdeen by the seine netters had a fantastic effect on **Peterhead**. The harbour trustees made them welcome, and built up a mighty infrastructure for the fleet. During the 1970s a new fish market was constructed.

58. Built in the 1930s, initially to accommodate steam drifters, the **Peterhead** slipway was in even greater demand forty years later. *Steadfast*, on the left, looks particularly ready for a repaint.

59. *Reliant* enters the water in the spectacular manner characteristic of launches from Irvin.

60. *Reliant* ran her trials on a day of rain and sunshine. The tall structure in the left background is the ice making plant which gave me various high viewpoints from where I took photographs of many other boats.

61. *Star Crest* receives her Caterpillar 565-horsepower diesel engine. Fishing was becoming more strenuous and greater power was needed.

62. Seen from the ice plant, ***Star Crest*** sets out from Peterhead.
She was known to be particularly capable when towing the big pelagic herring trawls.

63. *Star Crest* specialised in pair trawling for herring.
Sheathing at bow and quarter protected the planking when she was working the gear.

64. A basket of herring is swung ashore from *Star Crest* in dreich Mallaig weather. She endeavoured to follow the herring fishing for much of the year.

THE <u>NEW</u> SUPER-SUPER
HERRING PAIR TRAWL

on behalf of the makers APELDOORNSE of Holland

as supplied to STARCREST
(Skipper George Collin)

Outstanding characteristics of this net are as follows:—

* Forenet Mesh 48"

* Headline length approx. 38 fathoms.

This net covers a much larger fishing area than previous nets and the larger mesh reduces the water resistance.

We think this is the net of the future and wish Skipper Collin every success in his new venture.

65. Commercial businesses regularly placed advertisements in the weekly paper *Fishing News*.

66. *Ulysses* ran her trials one day and *Achieve* the next.
Irvin was busy. Already two more boats were under construction.

67. Green-hulled *Achieve* sets out for trials. She was built from the same hull moulds as *Ulysses*.

68. *Sunbeam* was built for a Lossiemouth skipper but landed her catches in **Peterhead**.

69. *Resplendent* and ***Sunbeam***, (foreground), are under construction amid temporary stays and shores and platforms. There were official rules for scantlings and materials and quality of build.

70. Gutsy and sizeable *Resplendent* can carry big catches. Seine ropes are stowed below deck in storage bins.

71. *Resplendent*'s low hard bilges are very noticeable.

72. A seine net catch is offloaded from *Resplendent* at **Peterhead**.

73. Wheelhouse fittings on board *Resplendent* included Elac LAZ71 echosounder, (left), and Decca Navigator (forward of the steering wheel).

74. *Graceful* departs for trials on June 25 1974.
Trials were necessary to check that all was working well before the boats were handed to their owners.

75. Skipper Philip Morgan had *Graceful* built as replacement to his earlier vessel of the same name, delivered in 1961 from Irvin.

76. It is a rainy windy day in **Peterhead**. *Daisy* nears completion.

77. *Daisy* runs her trials.
She carries her beam well forward and aft, but beauty of line is still a big consideration.

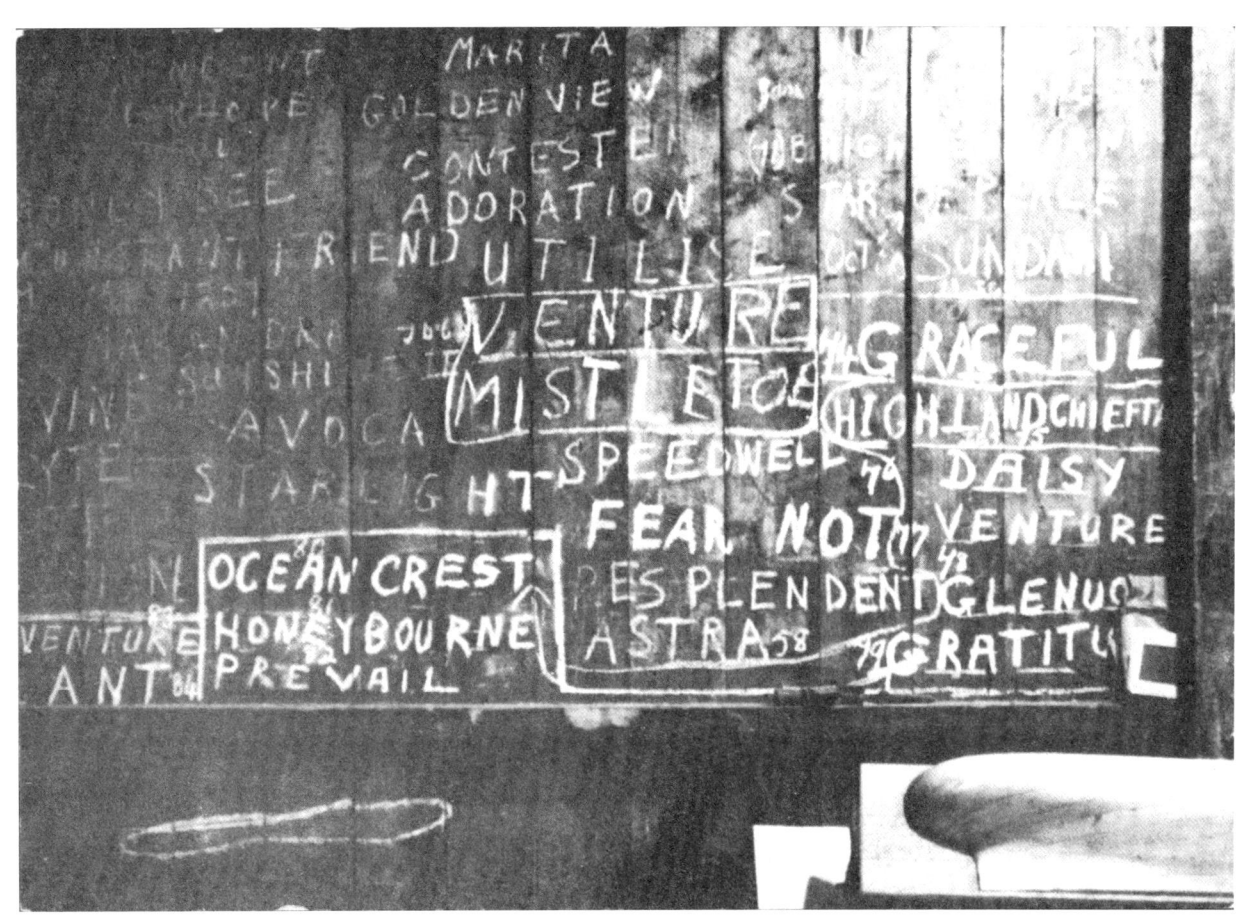

78. Poem / postcard *A Sea Street Anthology*
By courtesy of the Estate of Ian Hamilton Finlay.

79. *Replenish* and *Radiant Way* were the final two boats which Irvin built and fitted out simultaneously. Sometimes, in the past, two had been launched on the same day.

80. *Replenish* was the hundredth vessel constructed by Irvin since it began building steam drifters at Peterhead just around the start of the First World War.

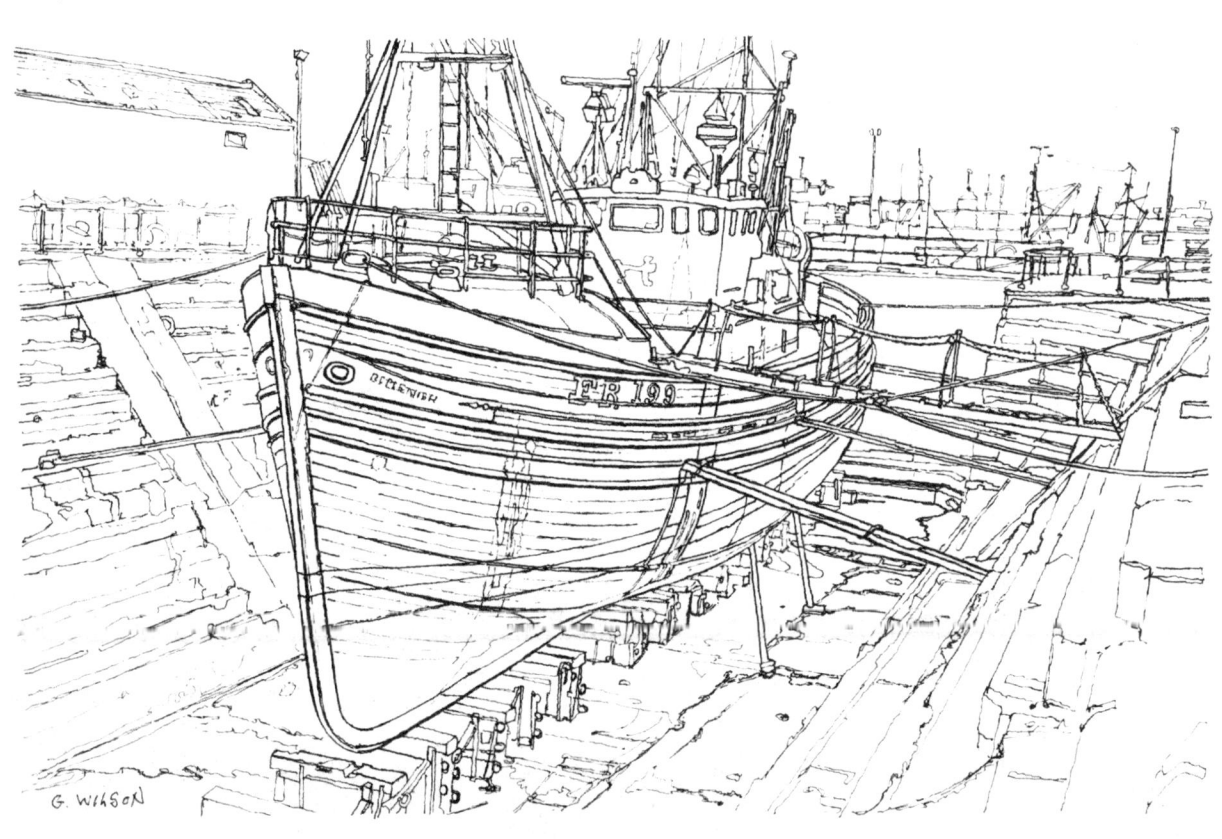

81. Within the structure and pattern of the dry dock in **Peterhead**, the superb shape of *Replenish* can be fully appreciated.

82. *Radiant Way* is another big, competent and workable boat, but her completion leaves the Irvin order book empty.

83. Delivered early in 1976, ***Radiant Way*** was the penultimate boat from Irvin.

84. Built in 1954 as *Trustful II*, and similar in hull form to *Silver Hope*, ***Duncairn*** was happily picking away at the seine net fishing some twenty years later.

85. For a short while, *Constant Friend* worked Scottish flydragging seine nets from **Brixham** in Devon.

86. *Sunbeam* INS189 was the final vessel built by Irvin. After her completion, the firm continued with repair work for some years.

87. **Sunbeam** was the only Irvin boat to be fitted with a deck shelter at the time of her completion. It gave crewmen a modicum of cover when handling the catch.

88. In 1979, during her first full year of fishing, *Sunbeam* was the second highest earning flydragging seine netter in Scotland.

89. Boxes of fish, well covered in ice, are put ashore from *Sunbeam*. Rope storage reels rendered flydragging seine net fishing safer for the fishermen.

90. On June 15th 1979 *Sunbeam* was the first boat to land a catch into a new extension to **Peterhead**'s fish market.

91. Designed for seine net fishing and herring drifting, ***Rambler Rose*** was the first fishing boat built by Irvin following the Second World War. She ran her trials in very heavy weather.

92. Irvin acted as fish selling and management agents for many boats including traditional seine netters, and also owned a number of them in partnership with skippers and other shareholders. Note the Irvin name on the boxes *c*1972 here in Peterhead.

93. In 1972 **Aberdeen** was still the most important Scottish port for demersal fish landings, most of which came from deep sea trawlers.

94. Aberdeen fish market in the early 1970s was an exuberant place and shrieked with gulls. These trawlers were known as 'side-winders', and hauled their nets over the side rather than up a stern ramp.

RICHARD IRVIN & Sons Ltd.

───── NORTH SHIELDS ─────

Telex: 537009   Telephone: 70225

───── & ABERDEEN ─────

Telex: 537007   Telephone: 52651

FISHING VESSEL OWNERS, FISH & HERRING SALESMEN AND SHIP'S STORES MERCHANTS

BLACKSMITHS, SHEET METAL WORKERS AND CARPENTERS, RIGGERS AND NET MANUFACTURERS

Also at

PETERHEAD (Tel. 2044)   FRASERBURGH (Tel. 3102)   BUCKIE (Tel. 3286)

LERWICK (Tel. 1264)   MALLAIG (Tel. 2343)

Wooden Fishing Vessels built and repaired at Shipyard, Peterhead

95. As shown by this advertisement, published in *Fishing News* on October 5th 1973, Irvin had wide fishing interests. About this time, nevertheless, it invested in oil- and gas-related opportunities, and in 1997 withdrew from the UK fishing industry.

Afterword: Contradistinctive

Late in 1972 Irvin took delivery of the 152ft 9in, welded steel, stern trawler *Ben Asdale* A328 from Dieppe builders Ateliers et Chantiers de la Manche. I took photographs of her at sea off Aberdeen in mellow soft-hued light shortly after her arrival from France.

Stern trawlers hauled the net up a stern ramp, and the catch was spilled through a hatch and processed under cover. *Ben Asdale* had a British Polar 1800hp engine with controllable-pitch propeller. Prior to 1969 British stern trawlers were designed for demersal fishing only, but *Ben Asdale* had the necessary higher engine and winch power to work enormous pelagic trawls also. She made trips as far as the cod-rich Barents Sea to the north-east of Scandinavia, and fished for much of the time under Skipper John Gowie, and brought back her catches chilled in ice.

In appearance, *Ben Asdale* was a counterpoint to the curvilinear timber-hulled cruiser sterned seiner trawlers. She represented a different flow of ideas. There were those who thought her purely functional in looks, somewhat un-poetical. But to me she was contradistinctive, quite striking, composed of angular shapes which made a bold statement.

There was a dark and poignant side to *Ben Asdale*. Late in 1978 she took part in the mackerel fishery off south-west England. Just after she had transferred a twenty-two-tonne catch of mackerel into a Russian factory ship in Falmouth Bay on December 30th, it was found that her steering gear would not work. Her anchor was dropped, but it failed to grip. She was swept onto rocks in a ferocious Force 10 gale and became a total wreck. Three men lost their lives.

Acknowledgements

I would like to thank all the kindly and supportive people who provided the information which has enabled me to put this book together. It is impossible to mention them all individually because there were so many of them.

Special thanks must go to all associated with Richard Irvin & Sons Ltd., and to the skippers and crewmen on board the beautiful boats built at the company's Peterhead yard.

My involvement with the fishing and boatbuilding communities has been a rewarding and happy experience.